C. H. (Charles Harold) Herford

The Essential Characteristics of the Romantic and Classical Styles

Styles

With Illustrations From English Literature

C. H. (Charles Harold) Herford

The Essential Characteristics of the Romantic and Classical Styles
With Illustrations From English Literature

ISBN/EAN: 9783337008222

Printed in Europe, USA, Canada, Australia, Japan

Cover: Foto ©Thomas Meinert / pixelio.de

More available books at **www.hansebooks.com**

THE

ESSENTIAL CHARACTERISTICS

OF THE

ROMANTIC AND CLASSICAL STYLES:

WITH ILLUSTRATIONS FROM
ENGLISH LITERATURE.

BY

C. H. HERFORD, B.A.

TRINITY COLLEGE.

BEING THE ESSAY WHICH OBTAINED THE MEMBERS' PRIZE, 1879.

Vis superba formae.

CAMBRIDGE:
DEIGHTON, BELL AND CO.
LONDON: GEORGE BELL AND SONS.
1880

THE

ESSENTIAL CHARACTERISTICS

OF THE

ROMANTIC AND CLASSICAL STYLES:

WITH ILLUSTRATIONS FROM ENGLISH LITERATURE.

BY

C. H. HERFORD, B.A.

TRINITY COLLEGE.

BEING THE ESSAY WHICH OBTAINED THE MEMBERS' PRIZE, 1879.

Vis superba formae.

CAMBRIDGE:
DEIGHTON, BELL AND CO.
LONDON: GEORGE BELL AND SONS.
1880

TO

MY AUNT

MRS TURNER

OF NOTTINGHAM

μικρὰ ἀντὶ μεγάλων.

PREFACE.

THIS Essay is published in compliance with the conditions under which the prize is awarded. Without at all wishing to deprecate criticism, I may plead this claim to some degree of indulgence, that it was composed in odd hours snatched from severer work during the few months preceding a Tripos.

CONTENTS.

PAGE

Chap. I. INTRODUCTORY: CLASSIC AND ROMANTIC IN GENERAL 1

II. PRINCIPLES OF STYLE EXEMPLIFIED IN VERSE . 22

III. STYLE AS MATERIALLY AFFECTED: REALISM . 29

IV. STYLE AS FORMALLY AFFECTED

(i) BY EMOTION 41

V. (ii) BY FANCY 57

VI. (iii) BY SENSE OF MYSTERY.

CONCLUSION 67

CHAPTER I.

INTRODUCTORY. CLASSIC AND ROMANTIC IN GENERAL.

§ 1. THE symbolic nature of the words current in the complexer departments of thought is nowhere better exemplified than in those which serve as the badges of literary movements. Literature is so intimately concerned with all the faculties of man, that every literary work presents a variety of aspects which, though without any essential connection, are easily associated. And thus the application of terms which properly, it may be, denoted only one of them, ramifies in all directions, and their connotation becomes vague and indeterminate. Of this familiar process the terms Romantic and Classical are famous examples; the former more especially, which, from its original precise reference to the mediaeval epics written in the Romance tongue, was first transferred by the French novelists of the 16th and 17th centuries to fictitious works in general, assumed thence a still more vague reference to that sort of charm in reality which suggests unreality: and now

retains the faintest possible flavour of this sense as a
stock term of the guide-book and the advertisement.
The Romantic school of the beginning of this century
gave the term a more distinct reference to the past,
but the implication of any special period became
continually less exclusive as their poetic culture grew.
Alfred de Musset has amusingly illustrated[1] the
confused associations of the term, and the perplex-
ities of his worthy provincials have probably been
experienced, in a degree, by every serious critic.

The history of the term Classic is scarcely simpler.
From its original reference to the first class of
Roman citizens, it was in late Latin transferred to
those whom, by a less definite metaphor, we too
entitle first-class writers. Deference to the literary
authority of antiquity long made the term a synonym
for the writers of Greece and Rome ; and this, in
spite of the constant extension of the word to some
whom modern criticism recognises as their equals, is
still, when used absolutely, its commonest application.
Let us attempt to clear this indefiniteness.

§ 2. We will, in the first place, notice an
especially confusing ambiguity in the usage of these
terms, Romantic and Classic.

They denote on the one hand two types of poetic
mind or of poetry, on the other, two movements
based upon the imitation or revival of these types.
In the same way the familiar contrast of Platonist

[1] *Lettres de Dupuis et Cotonet.*

and Aristotelian may either refer to certain schools
of mediaeval logicians or Renaissance moralists who
consciously derived from the Greek thinkers their
method or their point of view; or it may be applied,
as by Coleridge, to express a broad distinction in the
speculative attitude of men, of which the relation of
Plato to Aristotle is not the source but the type.   In
this general sense we oppose the Romantic genius of
Shakspere to the classic genius of Sophocles : in the
special sense the Romantic school of Hugo, of Tieck,
of Coleridge to the classic school of Racine, Boileau
and Pope.

Hence Classicism and Romanticism suggest indif-
ferently the two sets of associations typified by Plato
and the Platonisers, by the Attic and the Atticist, by
the antique and the antiquarian, the child and the
lover of childhood, the naïve and the sentimental,
reality and reminiscence.   Both suggest the healthy
and vigorous emotion of youth; both the exaggerated
susceptibility of retrospective age.   The full power of
mature genius, which from one point of view appears
eminently classic, would be equally claimed by the
Romantic on the strength of his divinity Shakespere;
while the morbid extravagance of coterie sentiment—
the *Kranke*,—the *Alterthümelei*, with which Goethe
taunted the Romantics of his nation, are matched by
the no less provincial limitations of the French and
English schools of classicism.   Each party, in fact,
comprises in its own belief all that is most worthy

and permanent in literature; each to the other is a narrow and provincial sect, a wave which stirred the literary waters for a while, and then was lost. And there is no doubt that the battle of the schools is long past; and that as conflict had brought the contrasted methods into sharper contrast[1], so time blended them in a higher unity, from which, as a loftier stand-point, the former combatants look back, and recall with a certain disgust the vain noise and tumult, the personal rancour, the storms in the press, the battles in the theatre. "Ainsi," said Victor Hugo, " ces miserables mots, Classiciste et Romanticiste, sont-ils tombés dans l'abîme de 1830, comme gluckiste et picciniste dans le gouffre de 1789. L'art seul est resté[2].

I shall not at present anticipate the question what is permanent, what fleeting, in their opposition. In any case the essence of the Romantic must be studied through the eyes as it were of the Romantic school. The distinction was drawn by them, applied by them; and neither the connotation nor the denotation which they gave to the term can be fully understood without thoroughly entering, in the first place, into their point of view.

§ 3. Perhaps all violent movements are partly

---

[1] *E.g.* the conception of Classicism as involving strict obedience to canons was certainly intensified by the emphatic scorn of them expressed at first by the Romanticists. Cf. Ste. Beuve ' *Qu'est-ce qu'un classique?*' *Causeries du Lundi*, iii.

[2] Preface to *Marion Delorme*.

negative; they involve, that is, mingled with their
definite aim and purpose, a certain element of blind
revolt. They partly know what they seek, and
partly know only what they shun. And whenever
this is so, the directions which they take when
released from all restraint and bidden to seek their
ideals at will, are various and even discordant.
Those whose aims are mainly negative, find satisfac-
tion in whatever is opposed to the object of their
antagonism; they revel in a boundless field in which
every thing is new, and, by its mere unlikeness to
the old, delightful. They display an abnormal and
uncritical receptivity, an excessive and childish
capacity of pleasure. Such is the case with the
anti-classical reaction. A prosaic century had
passed away, which, after compassing by the pens
of encyclopædists the destruction of loyalty, religion
and poetry, and depreciating that mediaeval age which
was a chief example of all of them, had finally put
its principles into act, slain its king, made Reason
its God, and, with a formal abandonment of the
past, had inaugurated a new era. Such was the
passionate indictment of the reactionists. But there
were many who, however they might superficially
applaud the course implicitly enjoined in that indictment, at bottom only knew that they hated
conventional poetry, and conventional life; and
whatever was rare, poetic and unconventional,
whether in the Middle Ages or elsewhere, that they

were ready to glorify and to imitate. The Elisabethan Age of England, too much imbued with the
Renascence for naïveté, too little for pedantry; the
contemporary drama of Spain, brilliant with the
versatility of Lope and the catholic chivalry of
Calderon; the mediaeval epics of France and Germany,—Lancelot and Renard, Roland and the Nibe-
lungen; the stranger legend world of the Norsemen;
the mysterious figures of the Gadhelic legends,
represented as was then supposed in Ossian : the
mythology of the Greeks, familiar enough as a mine
for allegory and allusion but neglected as poetry :
the lyrics of the Jews,—little known, or read as
theology rather than as literature; all these, and
even the more remote treasures of Arabia, Persia,
India and China, were studied with eager and often
uncritical enthusiasm within the first 30 years of
the present century. Herder, with his manifold col-
lections of the lyrics of early literatures, had done
in a more cosmopolitan field what Percy did for
the ballads of England. Lessing had shewed his
countrymen the nobility of Homer and of Shakspere.
Goethe applied his plastic imagination to the construction of West-Oestliche Divans or caught and
perpetuated the last breath of true chivalry in Götz
von Berlichingen. Naturally influences so various,
whatever community of attraction underlay them, in-
duced considerable variety of literary style. Within
the range of lyric poetry, three distinct models

produced as many schools: the stern simplicity of
the north, the melodious sweetness of the south,
the brilliant fancy of the east, each had its devotees.
Uhland and Tieck stand apart almost as the Teuton
from the Italian.   So, the lyric measures of the
Spanish drama were of a different genius from
the simpler yet more dignified iambic of the Elisa-
bethans.

§ 4.   It would appear to be mere pedantry to
attempt to discern among these manifold tendencies
any one definite direction.   They are united in
divergence, but it is misplaced subtlety to unite
them in convergence.   All literatures except the
present, all styles except the conventional, seem in
favour: if nature is glorified here, art is extolled
there: if the gloom of the north bewitch these, those
are allured by the brilliance of the south, or the
luxuriance of the east.   I shall therefore simply
draw out certain forms of the movement which I
conceive to have an equal right to inclusion in it:
and by analysing the several modes of negative
revolt evolve the corresponding objects of positive
aspiration.

§ 5.   We may discern, as the first mode of the
Romantic, an attraction to a sensuous, vivid, fantastic,
even unreal, art.   For art is certainly regarded with
favour, however surprising it may appear, even by
the opponents of an artificial, if not artistic, poetry.
But then, it would seem, the art must be of a far

different genius: it must be the art which beguiles
the senses by variegation, not that which charms the
intellect by symmetry, the art which relieves the
monotony rather than the disorder of the world.
The Romantic poet, weary of the drab hues of the
age of understanding, turned to the brilliance of an
age of fancy, and in his impatience of the rationality
which he called impiety, and of the order which he
called routine, was the better pleased if the colours
were overcharged, and the forms out of drawing.
Every analysis of the movement must recognise as
an element in it a certain caprice or waywardness
of taste, which is attracted less by the intrinsic
charm of beauty than by its incidental unreality.
The wilfulness of defiance, now petulant now sportive,
mingles with the single mind of art.

An important element of this tendency to the
arbitrary or fantastic is the love of *contrast*. Unity,
subordination, harmony, are among the most obvious
attributes of classicism: diversity, picturesqueness,
and a sort of emulous self-assertion of each part, are
conventionally assigned to the Romantic. This has
in fact been regarded as the very centre of the
antagonism by one who, if not the leading poet of
the Romantic school of Germany, was certainly its
greatest critic and its most refined translator—
August Wilhelm Schlegel. "The whole play of
vital motion" he says in the first lecture on the
Drama "hinges on *harmony* and *contrast*. Why

then should not this phenomenon recur on a grander scale in the history of man? In this idea we have perhaps discovered the true key to the ancient and modern history of poetry and the fine arts. Those who adopted it gave to the peculiar spirit of *modern* art, as contrasted with the antique or classical, the name of *Romantic.*"

But though Schlegel lived to see the movement which he had helped to guide in Germany ebb out or lose itself in more catholic tendencies of art, at the time he wrote his lectures (1811) its growth was still incomplete in England, and was quite incipient in France. He could not yet entirely compass tendencies which, as they assumed the same name, cannot for us be separated from it. I accordingly admit this as perhaps the most important canon of the Romantic ideal in art, but still not as entirely comprehensive.

§ 6. Dissatisfaction with the contemporary world may find refuge in another way. Instead of seeking arbitrary and eccentric combinations of sensuous forms, it may fall into the point of view of the mystic, and inform even the naked prose of common life with a mysterious charm, by regarding as the veil of something which is not seen all that we see. Instead of rejecting the repulsiveness of reality, it may dissolve it in the glamour of symbolism : instead of resisting or forgetting, accept and idealise it. A more spiritual side of the movement

comes out here; with as close an affinity to religion,
as the former has to the sensuousness of art. Poetry,
which can represent both, shews here marked traces
of the former, and the poetic faculty is assimilated to
the inspiration of the prophet, instead of to the skill
of the artist[1].

It is easy to see how those dominated by this
sense of mystery should be especially attracted to the
religious and superstitious attitude of the naïve mind,
and especially of the mediaeval mind. Hence Romantic poetry is as essentially mysterious as it is bright
and fantastic: the suggestiveness and infinity of gloom
belong to it as much as the finiteness and completeness of colour. The shadowy depths of the forest,
haunted with gnome and dwarf, the lonely mountain
in whose side Barbarossa has his palace, and where
his horses pant impatient for the night-hunt, these
belong to one side of the Romantic genius; to the
other, the gay pageantry of chivalrous war and the
brilliant posing of Provençal love.

These two sides of the genius of Romance may
without excessive refinement be described as respec-
tively northern and southern. The Teutonic spirit
indeed enters into both, just as the Teutonic race was
largely mingled even with the races which spoke the
Romance tongues. But in the south, the bright-

---

[1] E.g. Novalis considered that 'der poetische Sinn mehr Ver-
wandschaft mit dem Sinne für Weissagung, mit dem religiösen,
dem Wahnsinn hat.'

ness of nature inspired a sensuous and gaily-coloured poetry and Arabian influence—to which the Troubadours owed not a little—encouraged this tendency, and stimulated an ornate and elaborate style of art: while the self-asserting individuality of the Teuton enhanced an unreserve in expression which the moderation of Greek genius, quick and southern as it was in emotion, had forbidden.

Mystery on the other hand is pre-eminently a Teutonic quality. Doubtless the thought of all peoples is at a certain stage penetrated by the instinctive conviction that what they see is a veil of something they do not see: and the Aryan peoples, more especially, share in common a mythology whose essential quality of mystery no one of them entirely overcame. The worship at Eleusis was as mysterious in our sense as in the more special meaning of the Greek; the rites of summoning dead spirits are impressive even in Aristophanes, and those of recalling a faithless husband still retain an element of weirdness in the disillusioned age of Theokritos. But neither Greek nor Roman retained so fully as the Teutonic peoples the genuine sentiment of the mysterious. The Greek was too plastic, the Roman too prosaic. The former embodied so vividly that something which he felt informing the things he saw, that the impressiveness of the unknown forsook it, and it assumed almost the familiarity of sense. In the latter, on the other hand, the intuition of the unknown had so little persistence that he readily dropped the whole scheme of thought which implied it, and retained an Olympus of empty names, supplied, by the ambition of political aspirants, with a ritual no less empty. Thus the frank imagination of Greece, intolerant of the obscure, impatient of the formless and the indistinct, tended almost as much by assimilating the unknown as did the dull imagination of Rome by relinquishing it, to destroy the mysterious. Only when the Teuton broke in upon their decaying splendour and power, with his persistent assertion of an ideal world and his defective plastic power of representing it, was the sense of the mysterious thoroughly developed: only then was that union of light and darkness, that twilight of imagination which lies between perfect clearness and complete unconsciousness, at length realised. Greece was like the radiance of midday, which as with a bold chisel determines and completes whatever is vague and incipient: Rome the total darkness which excludes even the suggestion of form: while to the Middle Ages belongs that hour of dusk when every shape at once prompts wonder and refuses to gratify it, a symbol and a veil, a union of inexhaustible suggestiveness and inexorable limitation.

§ 7. The ideals just characterised as the fantastic and the mysterious comprise between them a large part of what is strictly Romantic. To aim

at these qualities was to be unreservedly Romantic.
We have now to examine two movements which as a
part of the anti-classical reaction were really more
important than these, and which though indifferent
or even hostile to Romanticism in one aspect, in
another formed part of it, and gave a characteristic
turn to its literary creed.

Consider first the great and complex movement
towards *nature*.   It is essential to the comprehension
of Romanticism—more especially in France,—to
distinguish two currents as it were, in the stream,
which, at times blended, at other times appear
directly hostile.   Nature in poetry, nature in politics,—ardent idealism might suppose them the most
easily harmonised of ends : and yet their several
advocates could be separated by the whole difference
between the Revolution, and the reaction which half
overcame its ebbing tide.   To the men of the Revolution nature and freedom were synonymous; it
was Rousseau, its prophet, who had cried that in
this corrupt and civilised world man, naturally free,
was everywhere in chains.   To the men of the reaction politically indeed the 'state of nature' might
be full of bitter and repulsive suggestion : and they
sought to blot out the memory of it, by restoring
their nobles, king and Christianity.   But the very
ideal they sought led them back to the ages
when feudal power, if not unresisted, was on the
whole supreme, and when catholicism, if not un-

questioned, always got the better of its questioners. Here however they had a common stand-point with those whom purely literary sympathies were drawing that way. To revive the untrammelled realism of the ages which preceded Malherbe, to write with free obedience to impulse, to let nature create its own art, to speak without restraint of things which a simpler age was not yet so refined as to think un-poetical—in all this the pursuit of nature in litera-ture fell in with the reaction in politics. But on another side it no less obviously fell in with the Revolution. For what did this pursuit of nature mean but a revolt from the canons which since the 17th century had been observed in poetry, and whose authority had seemed to grow with their age?

From the double front which the literary move-ment towards nature thus inevitably assumed, re-sulted a similar diversity in the political and religious attitude which its members adopted. All with some-thing of revolutionary temper sought an ideal more or less associated with the past: but some, their temper associated with the political revolution: others their ideal allied to the political reaction. On the one side aristocracy, conservatism, religion; on the other, democracy, radicalism, scepticism. Here we find a reactionary noble like Chateaubriand or a feudal chieftain like Scott: there a Wordsworth or a Coleridge, opening their poetic careers with glowing tributes to the levellers of Paris. Here the

gift of poetry is assimilated to the religious ecstasy,
and its exercise leads a Schlegel and a Werner to
that church which was at once the most conspicuous
spiritual power and the most vital remnant of mediaeval life: there, Shelley is expelled from Oxford
for atheism, and refuses at the cost of a fortune to
recognise primogeniture. That mobility of political
principle which was not inconsistent with adherence
to artistic faith is especially seen in the history of
the French Romantic school. In the *cénacle* of
1827, ardour for literary emancipation was easily
combined with devotion to king and priest. Its
members could write enthusiastic defences of the
Bourbons and Catholicism with the same hands
which were consummating the revolt against the
canons and unities of classic prescription. It seemed
as if it were reserved for the very poets who appeared
to aim at restoring all that the Revolution had de-
stroyed, to destroy the single pillar it had spared.
And it is equally easy to see how when the change
came, their literary practice did not likewise suffer
revolution: how Victor Hugo for example could be
no less a leader in Romantic poetry after Ste. Beuve
had converted him (as he claimed) to democracy,
than when still full of the new wine of the Restora-
tion: just as, conversely, Coleridge could impress a
similar literary stamp upon the odes with which he
welcomed the Revolution, and on the too rare fugi-
tive pieces of the latter days when he 'sat upon

Highgate hill" the coryphaeus in England of mystic theology.

It will now be clearer what element the movement towards Nature, thus complexly related to the Romantic movement, contributed to it. It was the variety of nature unchecked by an eclectic art; the profusion of forms and colours, of lights and shades, ministering in every way to the love of contrast :— beauty mingled with ugliness, the strong with the weak, the graceful with the grotesque, the charming with the repelling, the grave with the gay. And thus we explain the apparent paradox that art and nature should be equally associated with Romantic poetry : that in one place there is nothing in nature, however perfect, that it will not alter, in another nothing, however monstrous, that it will not retain. Fantastic art and natural realism have both a share in it; it is at once ideal and real. It accepts the contrasts of nature, and where they are too delicate amplifies them by art.

Realism then may be laid down as the third mode of Romantic contrast.

§ 8. But yet another movement contributed indirectly to form the ideal of Romanticism. An age of deeper passion was come, and higher susceptibility to emotion naturally led to a higher estimation of it. Enthusiasm, depreciated by a Locke, a Shaftesbury, a Hume, was now assimilated to in-

---

¹ Carlyle's *Life of Sterling.*

spiration, and calm rationality to mechanical routine. The age of 'force' and 'genius' was at hand, with its Carlyles and Emersons, its exaggeration of the power of the individual, its neglect of the inertia of the race. Forcible individuality always tends to an infatuation of self-confidence. From its first naïve intuition that all men are possessed by its own ardour, it passes to an impatient recognition of an opposing world, which however it is confident of subduing: finally it seeks refuge from a hopeless struggle with the present in the image of an ideal past or future. The history of the German Romantic school distinctly exhibits these two latter phases. To idealise the real, to inform Philistinism with genius, to animate the dull mechanism of routine; to give to the stiff conventional outlines of the prosaic world they knew, the flow of beauty and the boldness of strength, to pervade with the spirit of poetry all ages, classes, employments, pursuits and relations; this was their great inspiration. They seized the less conventional sides of contemporary life, and invested them with an ideal dignity and significance. Thus Schiller in his early years glorified the forest-robber, and numbers of the German youth became Karl Moors in real life.

In the same spirit they naturally turned to those poets who had combined poetry with practical activity, like Dante, or with a common handicraft like Sachs[1].

[1] Gervinus, *Gesch. d. deutschen Literatur.*

They lingered over the traditions of chivalry, when the inspiration of the poet enforced the soldier's, and the baron's feast was incomplete without the minstrel's song. And naturally, as the task of transforming the inveterate prose of the present appeared more and more impossible, they assumed with the more fixity a retrospective attitude. In a word, the mediaevalism already prompted by Catholic sentiment, and aversion to Aufklärung, was reinforced by the enthusiasm of poetry.

It need hardly be pointed out how other kinds also of powerful sentiment, repelled by uncongenial realities, sought refuge in the same direction; how the story of Dante was cherished for its mystic love, that of S. Louis for mystic religion: how a more sensuous passion lingered over the tale of Abelard, the legend of Lancelot; and how the very extravagance of chivalrous love, which could worship a name and search through Europe the owner of a face on a locket, powerfully attracted men weary of the less ideal and—in the conventional but here not inapt phrase—the less *romantic* affections of their day.

It is clear then how the wave of tenser emotion which broke upon western Europe towards the end of the last century fell in with the other influences which promoted a retrospective culture. It is obvious also in what direction it would revolt from the classic models of style. The unrestrained utterance of passion, the sympathetic diffuseness of the naïve narrator and even the prolix enthusiasm of the less inspired ballad-maker, now commend themselves to the poet as precious qualities of poetry. Sentiment, however obtrusive, is never coldly received. The drama of Schiller is in fact typical of this side of Romanticism, as Shakspere's is of its inexhaustible variety. When Schiller blamed Shakspere for the "coldness with which he can joke in the midst of tragedy," he was really dividing Romanticism against itself; he was arraying sentimentality against the abruptness of contrast which apparently, though not necessarily, excludes it. This is one of the inevitable paradoxes of the subject.

§ 9. The above review, though ostensibly confined to the Romantic, has already indicated by implication, the qualities to be regarded as classic. Classicism opposes to the arbitrariness of fancy a pervading rationality; to the mysterious the intelligible: to the unpruned variety of nature the limitations of an eclectic art: to passion glorified and dwelt on, passion restrained and somewhat disparaged. Romanticism, on the other hand, makes prominent the qualities conspicuous in the youth of a nation; bright aimless fancy, awe of the unknown, eager uncritical delight in the abundance of nature; impetuous joy and sorrow, breaking forth into such free and instant tears and smiles as the Argonauts

uttered, or the comrades of Odysseus. In Classicism
an age of understanding and refinement severely
asserts its rights: and excludes whatever cannot be
brought to its test; all that is obscure, redundant or
defective, too prominent or too unobtrusive for its
part, or which suggests undignified or repellent associations. Unity of form is blended with eclecticism
in subject; the taste of an exclusive age is seen in
the choice of the latter, that of an intellectual age
in the treatment of the former. Of these two elements
the exclusiveness tends with the growth of a more
catholic culture to diminish, while an enlarged
understanding becomes capable of imposing a unity
not less complete but only more complex upon more
diverse matter. And thus the antagonism of the
two movements tends, as has been said, to dissolve,
the more permanent elements of each persisting,
while the more transitory drop out. The wide
outlook of Romanticism is accepted by a new gene-
ration which at the same time rejects its wilful
eccentricities. The nature, the passion, the mystery,
the grotesqueness and the repulsiveness which it
freely admitted are no longer ejected absolutely
from the palace of art. Neither, however, do they
any longer enter it like a motley and disorderly
throng, where each thrusts himself forward and
speaks as of equal right at equal length. They
appear rather as members of an organic whole where
each has a function which he neither exceeds nor

falls short of; where one is the central dominating figure, and another appears for a moment, to speak a line.

These then are what is permanent in the principles of Romantic and Classical art, and which, like whatever else is permanent, cannot ultimately conflict. Each school seized upon a fragment and exaggerated its value: only when the fragments were combined in a higher synthesis could the complete sphere of art be formed.

CHAPTER II.

PRINCIPLES OF STYLE EXEMPLIFIED IN VERSE.

§ 10. THE structure of Verse may be regarded as the most external and formal part of style. The principles it involves are few and obvious, and its character is for the most part stamped upon its face. It will therefore be well to begin with a brief discussion of Romantic and Classical verse, on which the essential marks of the two styles are impressed in a manner elementary, yet clear.

To begin with the latter. According to the previous discussion, we may expect a verse marked by conscious, deliberate and studious art, as the fruit of a Humanist age that glories in man, and in whatever is most distinctive of man; a verse reserved in the expression of the more naïve and unconventional qualities, and anxious not to betray enthusiasm (in the 18th century sense) by running out of bounds; a verse, moreover, symmetrical rather than various, partly from a general preference for the former quality, and partly from the disposition to make it predominate in the more external and formal sphere. All these qualities are embodied in the so-called heroic couplet, as used by the classicists of England. In one respect indeed this measure is less characteristically classic than the Alexandrine employed by those of France; inasmuch as its five accents fall less easily into a perfectly symmetrical line. This must in fact be regarded as an essentially Romantic element perpetuated by a national tradition too deeply fixed to be altered. The Classical poets, however, did their utmost to transform the foreign metal in which they were compelled to work, and to obliterate as far as possible all suggestion of their barbarous precursors.

Within the limits of the line, the rhythm had been unrestrained; they studied to make it frequently fall into two symmetrical movements. The iambus had been freely replaced by a trochee; they restricted this license within the narrowest limits. The sense had flowed habitually beyond the couplet: they made every couplet a unit in a symmetrical series. Double rimes had been commonly used, by Chaucer habitually; they banished them almost entirely[1]. Such irregularities in metre as the occasional Alexandrine and the triplet, which were mere excrescences in the genial luxuriance of Dryden's style, became conspicuous anomalies in the pointed artificiality of Pope's. They suggested the riotous excess of a genius too freely indulged, and in his later poems he wholly abandoned them.

---

[1] Pope's well known couplet about 'leather and prunella' is one of the rare exceptions.

§ 11. It is less easy to indicate any single rhythm which is exclusively or especially Romantic. As deviation is more manifold than conformity, the license of nature than the restraint of art, so the Romantic genius revels in a thousand forms, where the Classical perfects a few. We may however note two principal classes of form which are characteristic of it. The impatience of the ordinary, of the light and air of common day, which belongs to the Romantic genius, would find expression in a verse which either permitted, or by its very form involved, the utmost variety of effect. The blank verse of the Elisabethan, by its very freedom allowed the greatest diversity of rhythm, and lent itself with the utmost flexibility to every variation in the hue or the tension of emotion. The complex rimed stanzas of the Italians and Provençals, on the other hand, while they rather checked variety of rhythm, imposed by their very structure a variety more mechanical indeed, but at the same time more striking and emphatic. The one method, the more Teutonic and northern, has greater regard for the inner movement of thought; the other bears the more external and sensuous stamp of the south, using a feature of form which has least relation to the meaning. But the two types are intimately blended. As the Teutonic element in the races of Italy, Spain and France had influenced the literature of those countries, so England in turn blended the artificial Romantic forms with the more flexible indigenous ones. Chaucer had created by his French and Italian rhythms—especially the heroic couplet and the seven-line stanza—a powerful tradition, one too powerful for any of his successors, even the author of Piers Plowman, to overcome. Surrey and Wyatt natural-ised the sonnet, and Spenser the octrain, with a characteristic addition of his own[1]. He also gave brilliant treatment, in his lesser poems, to many other measures, *e.g.* six-line stanzas of different types (*Sheph. Cal., Jan. Oct. and Dec.*), the rimed couplet (*Ib. Maye, February, Mother Hubbard's Tale*), seven-line stanza (*Daphnaida*), and more complicated stanzas in the *Prothalamium* and *Epithalamium*.

And the blending of these two types of verse produced a third method of obtaining variety, still more specifically Romantic than either; that, namely, in which the inferior variety of the rimed and syllabic verse was brought into contrast with the greater variety of the native rhythm, by the use of a verse in which the former was normal, the latter habitual, so that every use of it caused a piquant irregularity which is essentially Romantic.

I have already noticed the changes which the classical poets introduced into the rimed couplet;

---

[1] The complex stanzas of *Ælla* and the *Battle of Hastings* (both versions) deserve mention by the side of Spenser's, who doubtless suggested them. Chatterton was probably beguiled by the affected archaism of Spenser into the use of stanzas as anachronous as his language.

changes which gave to rime an entirely different
artistic effect, significant of the new school of genius
it was to serve. For nothing can be more unlike in
effect than verse in which the sense runs freely on,
and that in which a pause at the end of line or
couplet is habitual. In the latter case the rime
coinciding with the divisions of the sense, only
accentuates its regularity : just as the recurring
strokes of the drum emphasise the regular march of
soldiers ; in the former, the very symmetry of the
rime throws off the unrestraint of the sense, as the
same drum heightens the effect of an irregular
march ; and the use which—beside Spenser—Shelley, Keats and Browning[1] have made of it, shews
that it is as capable of a Romantic as, in its more
familiar use, of a Classical effect.

In a similar way, every deviation from the normal
structure of verse, even by a nearer approach to
the unfettered language of prose, has an irregular,
piquant, and essentially Romantic effect : *e.g.*

> "And all the winds, wandering along the shore,
>   Undulate with the undulating tide."

In cases like this, the normal rhythm, running as
a sort of undertone in the imagination, sets off the
strangeness of the rhythm which meets the ear.
In prose, on the other hand, comparative irregularity

---

[1] *Epipsychidion, Endymion, Lamia, Sordello.* Cf. too the variety
of movements which Hugo and Musset introduce into the Alexandrine, still retaining the rime.

of rhythm is normal, and has the effect of regularity. Elisabethan blank. verse presents many other applications of this principle ; for example, the occasional half-lines[1], both within and at the end of a speech, and the irregular metre of lines broken by a pause. Of the former kind an example is—

> "The miserable have no other medicine
> But only hope :
> I've hope to live, and am prepared to die."
>
> > *Claudio*, in " Measure for Measure."

Of the latter, the famous passage in the same scene :—

> "Than the soft myrtle; but man, proud man,"

which Coleridge, always most subtle in discerning Romantic traits, so zealously defended[2].

The same character belongs—though in a less degree because less irregularity is involved—to the variety in degree of accent which marks the Elisabethan iambic. Of the five normal accents Shakspere frequently uses three only, as in

> A lócal habitátion and a náme...
>
> The lúnatic, the lóver and the póet...
>
> And dúty in his sérvice périshing...
>
> Make périods in the mídst of séntences, &c....

---

[1] Similarly it is essentially a Romantic trait to admire as such, what Dr Newman calls ' the pathetic half-lines of Vergil.' Which however the genius of classic art compels us to attribute merely to the absence of correction.

[2] *Lectures on Shakespere.*

In Pope's hands the exquisite variety of this movement was abandoned; and the accents of his normal
verse are both more numerous and more emphatic—
a natural consequence of the conciseness of epigram-
matic style.

Again, a still bolder variety may be obtained by
basing the rhythm on accents instead of syllables.
This, though certainly not of Romance origin, is
undoubtedly of Romantic effect; as Coleridge, who
introduced it (in *Christabel*), was the most genuinely
Romantic poet of the modern English School.

Finally, the whole system by which the Elisabethan dramatists mingled prose and verse, rime and
blank, epic and lyric, in the same play, is, to us at
any rate, Romantic. To them it doubtless had no
such force: but was simply the natural procedure
which permits different sides of life to be represented
in language appropriate to them: but the modern
has been familiarised with a severer and less prodigal
art, and to him this profusion of effects has a charm
more subtle and delicate than that of nature—
the charm of Romantic variety, irregularity and
contrast.

CHAPTER III.

STYLE AS MATERIALLY AFFECTED.—REALISM.

§ 12.   VICTOR HUGO, in the famous preface to *Cromwell* which served as the manifesto of the French Romantic school, declared that the epic was the peculiarly antique, the drama the characteristically modern, form of art.   The drama combines all elements of life,—body and mind, sense and intellect, grotesqueness and beauty.   Its ideal is to express character vividly, to accumulate individualities and emphasise differences, to bring the most varied material into sharpest contrast.   Now this was certainly not the aim of the classical drama: nay, if we apply Lessing's criticism on the relations of poetry and sculpture to the similar though narrower difference between descriptive poetry and dramatic representation, we shall allow to the language of the drama even a less degree of realism in proportion as its more direct action upon the senses reduces the limits within which realism is inoffensive.   But the Romantic was less sensitive on this head : he loved nature as such, and from a quite different but concurring cause, he also loved contrast.

Both influences combined to make the drama the most characteristic form of modern art. Apart from differences of subject, the epics and the odes of modern times are more or less consciously influenced by antique models. Tasso, Dante, Milton, Klopstock would have written otherwise without Homer and Vergil: Cowley, Dryden, Collins, Gray, without Pindar: but the drama of Shakspere is in form as unlike, as it was probably independent of, that of Sophocles.

To illustrate this realism, which we may now, without necessarily confining it to the drama, term dramatic, is the object of the present chapter. We may regard it under two aspects: first, the introduction of certain ideas—secondly their treatment, when already involved in the subject. The Romantic poet both admits an idea more freely, and brings it more vividly home to the imagination: the classic will either exclude it altogether, or, admitting it, veil its offensiveness. Romanticism, elsewhere seeming to slight reality, and to seek in gay flights of fancy, full of surprises and improbabilities, an escape from the pressure of custom, here appears to embrace with enthusiasm whatever is offered. It is now realist, as elsewhere idealist: and classicism, elsewhere opposed to it from the side of the actuality of nature, here confronts it from the opposite camp of the ideality of art. But the contradiction contains its own solution. The cause of both attitudes is the same. Nature combines the two ideals. Infinitely various and comprehensive, she at the same time moves with, ultimately, the utmost uniformity. When the Romantic adopts nature as his cry, he means its variety more than its regularity: and when he seems to abandon it, it is only that an element slighted before is now excluded altogether.

This appears in many modes. Its condition is, as I have implied, a certain transparency of style, which admits with no softening disguise many things which the conventional artist, from refinement, dignity or sensitiveness avoids—the common, the naïve, the archaic, the rude, the repulsive; or again, things which, while perfectly real and simple, or even because they are such, lie beyond his interest and sympathy. It is characteristic of the classical theory of style not to express these fully in the language even where they are involved in the matter. According to that theory style and thought are not essentially connected, the one following the other as the impression the mould, but are separate entities which may be cultivated apart and according to different laws.

To the Classic, style is like the loose cloak of the Greek, not following the contour of the frame, but flowing in independent beauty; to the Romantic, in the aspect of him which we are now considering, it is like the tight dress of the Elisabethan, displaying unreservedly every line, graceful or deformed, and almost organically responding to every motion. It may be the mere admissi·a of unconventional terms —such as the 'handkerchief' in Othello, which at its first performance before a Paris audience so violently stirred the old Adam of Pseudo-classicism—or it may be a colouring of expression, or again an effect· that dominates the whole style from its deepest to its most superficial elements.

I shall illustrate this under three aspects: the introduction of the naïve, of the repulsive, and of what may briefly be called the subtlety and minuteness of nature. For the most part I shall draw upon the writings of the modern Romantics—the instances of all in the writings primarily Romantic—*e. g.* the Elisabethan drama—being sufficiently obvious.

§ 13. A very few words will suffice to explain the attitude of Augustan classicism towards the naïve and the archaic. The era of ripe understanding could not sympathise with that of a simpler intelligence than its own. An age that feels itself to be final is impatient of one that is obviously incomplete; and hazardous as are assertions of so wide a scope, it may safely be said that the age of Augustan classicism or even the 18th century in general, did attribute to their state far more finality than any one now ventures to assert of the conditions of the 19th.

The temper of such an age excluded too the archaic turns which it afterwards became the creed

of a mediaevalising poetry to revive.   They bore the
musty odour of the past like the old manuscripts
which contained them; and were no more to be
introduced among the well-bred idioms of the
eighteenth century than the old crooked blackletter
was to be permitted to mingle with the clear and
elegant modern type[1].

In the modern Romantic school it is of course
necessary to distinguish between an archaism or
naïveté which is purely dramatic and one which is
the expression of the writer's own retrospective sentiment.   In Keats, *e.g.*, it is very largely personal.
In Chatterton, whose great capacity for imaginative
sympathy with the past was united with no touch
of Romantic *sentiment*, it is wholly dramatic.   In
Spenser,—whose Hobbinols and Colins[2] often forget
their archaism in sudden bursts of poetry,—it is
doubtless partly dramatic; but Spenser, unlike most
of his contemporaries, had something f the modern
Romantic sentiment; and his archaism reflects his
own imaginative delight in the past of chivalry, of
Arthur, of Roland, however inappropriate to such

---

[1] It is true that Pope in describing the self-criticism of 'the
men who write such verse as we can read,' bids them occasionally
  "In downright charity revive the dead :
  Mark where a bold expressive phrase appears,
  Bright with the rubbish of a hundred years ;
  Command old words that long have slept to wake,
  Words that wise Bacon or brave Raleigh spake."
But he can hardly be said to have acted on the injunction.

[2] A rustic nomenclature, which Pope takes credit for not
imitating in his *Pastorals.*

II.   3

an age may be the particular kind and degree of
archaism which he assumed. And Spenser, like
Chatterton, often belies the simplicity of the age
whose language he affects by an ornate splendour
of imagery hardly known before the Renascence.
Keats, too, in his *Eve of St Agnes*, and *Isabella*, con-
stantly suggests the tone of naive sympathy with
which Chaucer tells a pathetic story.   How pointedly
unlike the calm dignity of conventional narrative is
the opening of the former poem :

> " St Agnes' Eve! ah, bitter chill it was," &c.

and of the latter

> "Fair Isabel; poor simple Isabel!
>   Lorenzo, a young palmer in Love's eye,
> They could not in the selfsame mansion dwell,
>   Without some stir of heart, some malady:"

yet the intervals are short in which the rich imagination of the modern does not break through this
affected simplicity ; for example in the third stanza,
where the 'ancient Beadman' is described passing
along the dim chapel-aisle ;

> "And scarce three steps *ere Music's golden tongue
> Flattered to tears* this aged man and poor:"

a list of Shaksperian richness inlaid, like a 'patine
of bright gold,' in the simple language of Chaucer.

More purely dramatic is the exquisite simplicity
devoid of archaism with which Mr Browning can
inspire a childlike character; and notably his *Pom-
pilia*.   On the other hand, the naïveté of which
Wordsworth in his earlier days so eagerly made his
poetry the vehicle can only be called with a qualifi-

cation Romantic; it involves too largely for the most part that flavour of the modern age, which the Romantics sought to avoid. The realism of style which they extol relates only to a historical reality. Shakspere, in parts a decided realist, they accept because time has drawn a magic veil between, which to our eyes invests his grossest realities with something of ideality: but let another Shakspere treat the 19th century, as he treated parts of the 16th, and they would turn away with chilled admiration from a pencil whose perverse fidelity only made more vivid the conventionalities they loathed.

§ 14. As the Romantic admission of the naive offended the classical worship of intelligence, and its proneness to the mysterious the classical demand for intelligibility, so its acceptance of what is grotesque or repulsive outraged the classical requirement of elegance. The social contrast to which this opposition points, and on which it rests, is equally plain. The society of the salon, which while it delighted in a veiled meaning would tolerate neither a childishly simple, nor a mystically obscure one, was equally imperative in banishing the uncouth, the rude, the repelling.

In fact the modern Romantic admission of the repulsive rested on exceedingly complex conditions. It was partly due to that higher sense of beauty, which finds an aesthetic value in discord. It was not only an assertion of nature against the exclusiveness of an artificial society, but also an attack upon the imperfect aesthetic insight which made it exclusive. Revolt against the privileges of pure beauty as such, was added to disparagement of the kind of beauty which had hitherto alone enjoyed them. The artistic opposition of variety to monotony, the political opposition of the outcast to the privileged, the antiquarian opposition of mediaeval unreserve to modern refinement, the ethical opposition of mediaeval asceticism to modern hedonism; finally, the more general antagonism of power to the canors of a shallow taste,—all these are resumed and united in the modern Romantic admission of the repulsive.

In France Victor Hugo vehemently asserted its rights in art[1], and did not a little to put in practice his own precepts[2]. In England Wordsworth's famous preface, though written from a different point of view—the poetical value of the natural language of passion,—involved a similar admission of elements repulsive to conventional refinement. In Wordsworth, however, this aspect of the theory affected merely a phase of his poetry, which on the whole is marked by a classic selectness of phrase and thought. It is Coleridge above all,—Coleridge the self-chosen poet of the supernatural element in Romance,—who dared in the vividest and most searching words to portray things repulsive and horrible, holding his

---

[1] Preface to *Cromwell*.
[2] *E.g.* "La Légende des Siècles."

readers, as the Mariner held the wedding-guest,
spell-bound till they have heard every detail of his
'ghastly tale.'

> "The very deep did rot : O Christ
>   That ever such things should be:
> Yea, slimy things did creep with legs
>   Upon the slimy sea."

None of Coleridge's contemporaries approached him
here. Scott[1] had perhaps drunk not less deeply
of the Romantic genius; but his Tory attachment
to the past included a certain deference to the
literary tone of the 18th century. His eye was
caught by the brilliance of chivalry and the more
picturesque lights and shadows which checker High-
land life : but he shrank from offending the traditions of an elegant literature by exposing its more
savage aspects. Keats was too much in love with
pure beauty to lacerate his senses willingly with
unsightly images. It is characteristic of him that
in the description of the uncarthing of Lorenzo, in
Isabella, he breaks off suddenly :

> "Ah wherefore all this wormy circumstance ?
>   Why linger at the yawning tomb so long?
> O for the gentleness of old Romance,
>   The simple plaining of a minstrel's song!
> Fair reader, at the old tale take a glance,
>   For here in truth it does not well belong
> To speak ; O turn thee to the very tale,
>   And taste the music of that vision pale."

---

[1] This reference does not include the prose writings of Scott.

And he expresses elsewhere explicitly (*Sleep and Poetry*) the feeling implicitly contained here :—

> "Strength alone, though of the Muses born,
>   Is like a fallen angel: trees up-torn
>   Darkness and worms and shrouds and sepulchres
>   Delight it; for it feeds upon the burrs
>   And thorns of life: forgetting the great end
>   Of poesy, that it should be a friend
>   To soothe the cares and lift the heart of man."

This is another instance of the conflict of complex motives, which we have had to notice so often. The sense of beauty is partly attracted by the mediaeval, partly repelled by it.

It is in fact necessary to pass to an age in which the full realism of Romantic genius is not checked by conventional decorum, nor yet condemned by an over-acute sensibility. The poet who inspired Keats shrank from no unrefinement in the signs of his allegorical pictures : and it was naturally just this point which was chosen for parody by Pope, the typical poet of an age more tolerant of moral than of literary indecorum. It is needless to dwell upon the realism of Shakspere; whether the offence to a narrow aesthetic taste arise from something in itself offensive, as in Spenser, or from something made so by peculiar circumstances, as where a comic *motif* is intruded in the climax of a tragedy.

And as Pope has been mentioned, it is proper not to forget that, however coarsely Spenser might express his moral antipathy to abstract vices, Pode

without thought of parody entirely equalled him,
when uttering his literary antipathy to concrete
poets.   Hatred, the passion of the era of Augustan
classicism, produced in its poetry this troubled reflexion of Romantic qualities : and there is little to
choose in unrestrained virulence between (*e.g.*) Pope's
character of *Sporus* and Shelley's outburst against
Gifford in the *Adonais*, though the unrestraint of
the one is deliberate and classic, that of the other
impulsive and Romantic.   Realism that merely
offends an aesthetic susceptibility may be a proprium
of the Romantic poet : but if it will serve to give
sting to an insult, it belongs of right to the Augustan
classic who scarcely feels the laceration of his taste
in the gratification of his vengeance.

§ 15.   Finally I shall briefly illustrate what I
indicated above as realism in respect to the subtlety
of nature.   The French Romantic school in its early
days had a favourite word which seemed felicitously
to describe the quality they valued most in art ;—
ciselure.   It was a sort of watchword with them ;
they wrote it above their portal and forbade all to
enter who were ignorant of it.   The clear-cut deli-
neation they loved included two elements; to make
a vivid impression on the imagination, and to portray
nature with delicate and faithful pencil, not slurring
details in vague generalities, but rendering them in
all their complexity of line and subtlety of light and
shade.   No doubt here, as in the Preraphaelite move-

ment of painting, these two aims are inextricably blended: and I shall not dwell upon the distinction, which it is nevertheless important to remark. Take as illustrations these few phrases of Keats, which without fancy—(with that we are not here concerned)—vividly describe natural facts such as the classical poet, a humanist who cares for nature only in its relation to man, passes by with unconcern: 'the most patient brilliance of the moon,'—'the calm-throated nightingale,'—'cool-rooted flowers,'— 'minnows, staying their wavy bodies 'gainst the streams, nestling their silver bellies on the pebbly sand.'

CHAPTER IV.

§ 16. "ALLES Lyrische," says Goethe, "musz im Ganzen sehr vernünftig, im Einzelnen ein Biszchen unvernünftig sein." It has the touch of irrationality which belongs to the expression of imaginative passion. It may appear strange to associate, however remotely, with what is meaner than man, a mode of utterance which has given him the noblest poetry: nevertheless, it is true that the purely emotional element in lyric expression connects it, in so far, with that rude language of feeling which belongs to the lower animals rather than with the articulate language of thought which is confined to man. Doubtless the form in which these characteristics appear is complicated and disguised by the high development of articulate language. It is not indeed the actual means of expression which are analogous; for the high development of articulate language has almost wholly substituted the symbolic implication for the direct expression of feeling, and left to interjections, which alone now represent that function, merely a last despised chapter of grammar. It is rather in the characteristics which accompany the expression than in the means consciously adopted to mark it that the resemblance lies. These may be defined as *incoherence* and *iteration:* two features which doubtless often arise from other causes than strong feeling, but, on the other hand, are conspicuously avoided in the language of calm reason. To a large extent no doubt these disappear in all articulate language, which, so to speak, carries off the stress of feeling by giving it abundant scope : still, when the stream is strong it finds the artificial channel too narrow, and if it does not break out along the old · bed it at any rate overflows the new : the utterance may not degenerate into mere inarticulate cries, but it still retains some of the characteristics of such cries. There is incoherence when the poet is hurried along too vehemently to forge each thought into perfect form, and flings it impatiently forth, a glowing but unshaped mass. Iteration too belongs as peculiarly to the language of emotion as variety and development to that of thought. Incoherent by its impatience of the unessential, passion at the same time reiterates and dwells upon the essential. Reflective thought, on the contrary, avoids equally the incomplete and the superfluous.

Of this nature is the contrast of Classic and Romantic style as affected by passion. Incoherence is necessarily alien to that completeness of expression which leaves no gaps to check the interpreting mind : and redundance is no less foreign to the artistic instinct, which refuses either to add to, or without variation to repeat, what is already perfect. It is in fact in this region that the indictment by classic of Romantic art is made with most effect. Take first of all the case of mere literal repetition of a word or a phrase. This may be due to an impulse in which either the pathetic or the imaginative element of lyric inspiration preponderates. Here is an example from Keats[1].

> "O Melancholy, linger here awhile!
>   O Music, music, breathe despondingly!
> O Echo, echo, from some sombre isle,
>   Unknown, Lethean, sigh to us—O sigh!
> Spirits in grief, lift up your heads and smile;
>   Lift up your heads, sweet spirits, heavily."

One can fancy some Aristophanes ridiculing this pathetic Euripidean iteration, in the modern critical Dionysia of a Quarterly Review! Take again the iteration not of pathos but of impassioned imagination in Shelley's description of the "winged infant[2]:"—

>   " white
> Its countenance, like the whiteness of white snow,
> Its hair is white, the brightness of white light
> Scattered in strings."

The classical poet would have been content to

[1] *Isabella*, LV.
[2] *P. Unb.* Acts IV.

notify its colour once for all; the sensuous vividness
of the white colour would have no enthralling attraction to his pen; it forms indeed a part of the
picture, and he will not omit it; but for the same
reason he will not dwell on it, and this ample
utterance of an imagination at white heat appears to
him like the idle redundance of childhood.

> "Prune the luxuriant, the uncouth refine,
> But show no mercy to an empty line."

Often, again, stress of feeling produces, instead of
absolute repetition, diffuseness. And inasmuch as
every touch which does not add to the completeness
of the expression is redundant, we will begin with
those so-called enthusiastic epithets which, giving
no new information, merely emphasise the writer's
feeling. It is this transparent expression of sympathy or antipathy which gives some of its native
charm to the style of Chaucer and to that of Spenser,
this unreserved utterance of the poet's and artist's
admiration of things beautiful, strong and noble, his
repugnance to ugliness, his recoil before the horrible.
'Wondrous' and 'good,' 'fair' and 'lusty,'—'cruel'
'hideous' 'dreadful' are for ever on their lips. Such
words, when used not descriptively but emotionally,
are, from the standpoint of classical art, as superfluous as if a sculptor should write upon the brow of
his statue how much he admired it. Many similar
intrusions of the poet's sympathy abound in Spenser:
e.g. in narrative :—

"His harmful hatchet he hent in hand,
.(Alas that it so ready should stand :)
And to the field alone he speedeth
(Ay, little help to harm there needeth !)."

Or again there is the diffuseness, not as here of
comment or exclamation, but of needless detail;

"A hideous roaring far away they heard
That all their senses filled with affright;
And straight they saw the raging surges rear'd
Up to the skies, that them of drowning made affear'd."

The poet betrays his sympathy with his cha-
racters by dwelling on their fears. Here we may
descend to that meaner kind of diffuseness which
arises from no Spenserian enthusiasm but from the
mere storyteller's egoistic insistance upon every detail
of his tale. It is here that we are reminded of the
tedious narratives, happily parodied in the *Rime of
Sir Thopas*, of those less gifted ballad poets who
dissented from Dryden's opinion that 'a poet ought
to write all he *ought*, not all he *can*.' This careful
attention to the 'limbs and outward flourishes' which
do .*not* compose the soul of wit is characteristic of
Romantic poetry in feebler hands, while extreme
abruptness and obscure compression mark where its
bolder spirit has been at work. The very con-
spicuousness of this quality in the traditional poetry
gave it a factitious attraction to poets who admired
every thing old: and the writings of some of them,
who do not deserve to be called feeble, are pervaded
by it. Keats, for example, even in his strictly nar-

rative poems such as *Isabella* and *The Eve of S.
Agnes*, gives his Pegasus a very loose rein, and
suffers him to take a desultory course, many a time
lingering where the air is rich and the leafy growth
luxuriant, and rarely pressing on with the self-
restraint of a single purpose. Especially noteworthy
are the various ways of concluding a narrative or of
dealing with the mass of emotion which the climax
of a great action arouses. Two modes of accom-
plishing this are equally Romantic, and equally
opposed; a third, which is peculiarly classic, is unlike both. The Romantic of the diffuse type is apt
to treat the climax without special distinction, to
develop unessential consequences with superfluous
detail, and so to winnow away the excitement into
indifference. The Romantic of the intense type
again will hasten on to the close, and strip away
with fiery impatience all but the bare indispensable
framework of the structure. Witness the most ef-
fective close of Shelley's *Cenci:* where the climax is
only felt to be complete when the final exit startles
away any lingering expectation that the innocent
will still be saved. On the other hand, the pure
classic ideal of art, severely excluding weak effects,
yet exacting at the same time the utmost continuity
and completeness, rounds off the climax with touches
of paler but harmonious colour. Perfect examples
of this are found in some of the longer poems of
Mr Matthew Arnold. There is no dissolution of the

climax in *Sohrab and Rustum:* the situation of the supreme moment is not changed: and in the gathering night Rustum still watches, Sohrab still lies dead. Had the poem ended here, it would have had the abrupter effect which I have described. But then comes a picture of solemn and harmonious beauty,—the river Oxus rolling calmly along the lands towards the sea,—which, without obliterating the expression of the tragic picture which preceded, invests its stern outlines with a tender opalescence of gentler sentiment. Nor when Empedocles has leapt into the crater does any god or man appear to alter or to moralise his doom: only a brief lyric song rises up from the woods of Aetna far down, and then turning away from the fiery eruption, calls up the thought of Helicon with its sleeping birds and beasts, and Apollo and the Nine glistening through the balmy night. In both cases that which succeeds the climax does not attempt to continue it, but falls at once into an undertone of subordinate harmony, softening without effacing the effect.

§ 17. To consider now the *incoherence* of lyric expression,—the Biszchen unvernünftiges of Goethe's phrase. By this I only mean, as I conceive that he only meant, a tenuity, an impalpable fineness in the associations which guide the transitions, not the absence of such associations: a revolt from the laws of the understanding which is compatible with full allegiance to those of imagination. Abrupt expression of this sort might be compared with a broken bridge which checks the passage of the creeping thing but does not stay the bird. For illustration I shall in the first place refer to an influence which, contemporaneous only with the ἐπίγονοι of Romanticism and by no means confluent through its whole range with Romantic tendencies, deserves to be introduced, as a notable source and stimulus of imaginative intensity. It is a commonplace remark that the poetry of that era displays a new interest in external nature. What is more important to observe is that a change in the conception of nature accompanies the changed attitude towards it. It is not merely that nature receives a reverence very different from the qualified admiration of the Augustans, but that the whole form and body of it is as it were transfigured:—informed with the analogue more or less literal, of the force, the passion, the intense life of man. In fact this was the poetic side of a more widespread revolution. The teleological idea was yielding, if not yet to that of evolution itself, at least to conceptions well fitted to prepare the way for it. The thought of an inert matter modified from without was passing into that of an organism moulded from within. The spontaneity of vegetable and animal growth, anomalous on the one plan, became typical in the other. Life pervades all things: the inanimate seems impossible: rest is but the outer garb of internal activity; sleep the vesture of dreams, death the gate to a life freed from the limitations of individuality[1]. The motive is the same whether it appear in the guise of Shelley's materialism or of Wordsworth's pantheism.

It is clear that a conception such as this could not remain without effect upon a poetry so deeply implicated in the aspiration after Nature, and so largely composed of descriptions of it. A vivified nature suggested, if it did not involve, a corresponding vivification of language. When Paulina is found to live and breathe, she can no longer be spoken of in the terms suitable to a beautiful but inanimate statue. All those words then which have grown so vague that they no longer call up a vivid picture to the imagination but only serve as the imperfect symbols of mental algebra,—words which the classical poet employs complacently enough to portray a world which to him is scarcely more living than they—it shuns as the shadow of death upon a poetry which before all things exults and revels in its life ; in which every word must light up the mind with a sudden radiance, or thrill it with reverberations. This vividness may however have many degrees. A word may suggest an image which is more vivid than the prosaic word merely because more rare, or it may have the higher expressiveness which belongs to the description of a conventionally lower in terms

---

[1] Cf. Shelley's *Adonais.*

of a higher phase of force: when for instance, in that
profound negation of the absolutely inanimate of
which I have spoken, the idea of the motionless and
inanimate is instinctively enriched with the thought
of hidden pulsation, when the least hint of force is
transmuted into a conception of arrowy swiftness and
vigour[1], when any suggestion of motion grows at
once into a picture of vehement life.

Take again some of the ever-recurring metaphors
of the simpler kind; those for example to which is
chiefly due the mannerism that clings to Shelley's
style. The winds are often 'dim,' the wings of
spirits 'winnow' the crimson dawn, curses fall
'flake by flake,' the eagle is 'entangled in the whirlwind.' That highly Shelleyan line which closes the
third Act of the *Prometheus*

> "Pinnacled dim in the intense inane"

is also in various respects highly Romantic. Almost
every word pierces instantly to the imagination;
scarcely one would have been used in such a sense
by a classical writer. The entire conception would
have been alien to his celestial architecture; the word

---

[1] (Of earth). "Life pulses in the stony veins."
                              Shelley, *Prom. Unbound.*
"The crawling glaciers cut me with the spears
  Of their moon-freezing crystals."
                                        Ib.

dim, though involving no such subtle conception, has a certain association of mystery which belongs to no other word; and the idea 'intense[1]' is in a startling manner combined with the notion of 'inane.' What could be more remote from the negative conception of space natural to a conventional poetry, as the bare residue which survives the abstraction of all the most vital qualities of reality, than this epithet suggesting however remotely a universe in which there is no part that is not pulsing with life?

It is the more extravagant use of metaphor, especially, which produces the 'touch of irrationality,' the incoherence in the eyes of perfectly sane and prosaic reason, to which I have alluded. Even to put one thing for another, which is the character of all metaphor, to substitute for the literal picture of an object an image of something else more or less unlike it without hint or notice, is a procedure foreign to the wholly rational genius of prose. Simile, on the other hand, which does not substitute but compares, is certainly a more prosaic figure. Again, the breach of continuity involved in the single metaphor may be repeated where several are combined: a number of images flash upon the poet in succession; each is fixed upon the canvas with a rapid dash of the brush, and the effect is vivid and highly impressive to the imagination: but the transitions are abrupt and there is a want of light

---

[1] Cf. Mr Matthew Arnold's similar use:—
    "In the intense clear star-sown vault of heaven."

and shade. Take among countless examples this stanza of the *Adonais* (32):

> "A pard-like spirit beautiful and swift,
> A love in desolation masked, a power
> Girt round with weakness: it can scarce uplift
> The weight of the superincumbent hour.
> It is a dying leaf,—a falling shower—
> A breaking billow; even whilst we speak
> Is it not broken?"

Again, ordinary language appropriates, with often arbitrary taste, certain feelings to certain terms, and for the most part to such as are little capable of expressing them with subtlety. Every movement then involving a richer phase of the feeling creates, in the effort at expression, a disturbance in the meaning of the terms; it reaches out on all sides and usurps the vocabulary of kindred feelings. Music appropriates colour and light and shade, it can be picturesque and sculpturesque; while painting in its turn adopts tone and harmony from music. A similar process, but carried far beyond the boldest affectations of art-coteries, marks the Romantic effort to utter the new intensity of feeling which belongs to the era. The intoxication of music, especially, which poor inarticulate Caleb Garth could express no better than by a nervous scraping of his stick upon the floor, and which even cultivated language renders so feebly, breaks out in this poetry into the boldest and most luxuriant imagery. To Shelley the spirits appear 'wrapped in sweet sounds

as in bright veils;' to Keats delicious symphonies
bud and swell, and blow 'like airy flowers;' and in
the melody of the carillon Victor Hugo hears a
gay spirit descending 'vêtue en danseuse espagnole,'
a frail stair of invisible crystal.   Thus the conception
of a nature instinct with life led to modes of expression as unconventional, and hence within certain
limits as Romantic, as that conception itself.   From
another point of view—its close association with religious faiths,—a different conception of nature is
doubtless more Romantic : that in which

> " There's not the smallest orb which thou beholdest
> But in his motion like an angel sings
> Still quiring to the young-eyed cherubim."

Shelley's universe, informed with the impulsiveness
of man, and Shakspere's, animated by his religion
and power of song, are equally unconventional.   Both
are unlike the Kosmos of Pope, blindly obedient to
a law imposed from without, and subject to a unity
comprehensive enough to include as mere varieties
of progress all the apparent aberrations of human
will.   With him reason guides the whole, as with
them impulse or inspiration every part : and what
each discerns as the guiding principle of nature, he
honours as the sovran prerogative in man : Pope,—
harmony, order, art; Shelley, the impetuosity of
natural genius.

§ 18.   This contrast suggests a brief discussion
of two poets whose day fell midway between these

two extremes, and whose style accordingly displays
the complexity of a transition, at once suffused with
the receding and tinged with the rising light. The
poems of Gray and Collins unite the exquisiteness
and refinement of the classical genius at its best with
something of the true Romantic *abandon*, and more
which is no bad imitation of it. In general Gray
stands nearer in cast of genius to the school which
preceded him; he is colder and more antiquarian;
his happiest turns are often the result of research,
and if they have not also the air of research it is
because Gray's art was largely of that kind which
does not betray itself. Collins, on the other hand, a
man of feminine reserve rare in that age of worldly
poets, had more of passion and of mysticism, with
something of the obscurity and the extravagance of
a genius that rushes too fast and wanders too far.
The tastes of both had a decided affinity to the wide
literary sympathies of the Romantic movement:
Collins, like Victor Hugo, like Goethe, had his
oriental eclogues, and shows the mystic vein of
Romance in his ode on the superstitions of Scotland[1];
and Gray, who for his multifarious pursuits in
science and literature might be called the more
prosaic Goethe of a more prosaic society, wrote
odes 'from the Norse' with the same hand which
indited odes after Pindar.

Especially do they invite comparison in their use

[1] It is characteristic of his age that he still *calls* them superstitions.

of Personification. Both are somewhat prone to
throw about the abstractions in which they think
there is a factitious semblance of humanity. Both,
beside their formal odes to Liberty, Mercy, Adversity,
&c.—abound in minor instances of this transforma-
tion. But Gray too often uses in the process only
the simple devices of a capital letter and a personal
pronoun, faintly coloured by some simple and obvious
attribute. The 'sweeping whirlwind,' 'fierce war'
and 'faithful love,' 'Truth severe by fairy Fiction
drest,'—'cares' that are 'sullen' and Passions that
are 'frantic,'—such is for the most part the rather
factitious personification of Gray. Collins, though
with the same devotion to the world of abstractions,
endows them with more reality and draws them
with a more subtle fancy. His *Spring* 'with dewy
fingers cold' falls indeed short of the Romantic
boldness of Blake's—

> "O Thou with dewy locks, who lookest down
>   Through the clear windows of the morning, turn
>   Thine angel eyes upon our western isle
>   Which in full choir hails thy approach, O Spring."

Nor have the *Passions* quite the picturesque
glow of Spenser: they have however a refined
delicacy of imagination which neither Spenser nor
Blake so unfailingly exhibits, and at least a rela-
tive brilliance amid the somewhat sober hues of
eighteenth century poetry.

Personification is natural to the loftier lyric

poetry of all times, impelled to combine high and abstract thought with vivid, concrete form.   In Gray and Collins it is partly due to the influence of Pindar, partly to that of Spenser, the coryphaeus of English allegory.   In either case it must be regarded as rather a Romantic than a classical characteristic. It has an unreality foreign to the transparency of meaning and reluctance to employ a needless fiction, which are conspicuously classic.   Even Pindar's style, with its rugged abruptness, its forced expression, its startling surprises and sudden leaps through the universe of thought, must be called, in thus far —however strange it may seem—Romantic: and whatever associations may connect personification with the classical methods of art are due chiefly to the fact that this, like other products of a rich imaginative poetry, was adopted and consecrated by rhetoric; and having received that stamp of propriety became part of the recognized machinery even of conventional art.   In any case the classic poet, if he treated it at all, would adopt rather the style of Gray than that of Collins; he would use simple forms and pale colours such as present merely a fleeting suggestion of the life which is merely feigned, instead of raising a brilliant phantasmagoria of high-wrought allegory, which only emphasizes, by the seeming substantiality of these abstractions, the Romantic unreality of the whole.

CHAPTER V.

§ 19. The poetry of Gray, in which the lyric quality is, as we have seen, impaired by something of coldness and something of research, may serve to lead us from the discussion of style as affected by stress of feeling to consider the more distinctly arbitrary combinations of *fancy.*

The manifold sources of poetic pleasure affect us through two avenues. Recognition and surprise—the familiar and the novel, the revival of an accustomed delight, and the stirring of a new one,—poetry may strike either of these chords, and it is one of its greatest charms to strike them together. There must be something strange in the familiar, something familiar in the strange. Mere fulfilment of expectation, too, has often the effect of familiarity, even when that which is expected is itself strange, and non-fulfilment has the effect of strangeness, even when that which surprises is familiar. Some of the finest effects of art arise from these combinations, as when a familiar air occurs unexpectedly in the midst of strange music; or when a strain familiar in the past has been so long unexperienced

as to fall with some shock of novelty even upon an
ear prepared for it.   On the other hand, these two
kindred forms of strangeness instead of conflicting
may coincide: an effect at once strange in itself and
unexpected may interrupt the familiar and habitual.
In such cases the result may be piquant or crude,
stimulating or displeasing, according as the inter-
rupted effect was still pleasing or were become trite.
Truth and beauty, it is said, are the same: and it is
true, in so far as no beauty unrelated to what is most
permanent in life can have a permanent effect: but
then the permanent must mean that which to the
imaginative insight of the poet is such, and which
even he may not at all times equally discern.   In
this way the highest beauty has at once truth and
strangeness: it gives the delight of recognition, but
recognition which though immediate is unwonted
and delight which is mingled with and enhanced
by wonder.   But if the highest art reconciles this
opposition by blending the contrary effects, it is
characteristic of the two types of art before us to
incline to a more or less exclusive use of one or the
other.   Each suffers the defect of its quality; in the
one, strangeness is too little tempered by familiarity,
in the other, the familiar too little qualified by
novelty: and accordingly the originality of the Romantic is sometimes crude, the correctness of the
classic occasionally trite.

The characteristic of fantastic expression is a

certain gratuitous and as it were sportive exercise of
exuberant faculty.   Naturally this may be suggested
with every variety of force, from the delicate flavour
of artificiality which pervades many of Shakspere's
sonnets to the repelling extravagance of the so-
called Fantastic or Metaphysical school of the 17th
century.

Of a quality so familiar in literature a single
instance, for illustration, will suffice:—

> "When forty winters shall besiege thy brow
> And dig deep trenches in thy beauty's field,"

is a fair example (out of a thousand) of the fancy of
Shakspere at its normal level,—neither hard nor
extravagant, and with a touch of beauty as well
as quaintness; and it has that air of an inspiration
easily provoked to adventure and slow to return
from it which becomes so well the age of Eldorado
enterprise.

It is more worthy of remark that this quality
is, in a limited form, no less conspicuous in the
Augustan poetry.   In the *Pastorals* of Pope, for
instance,—a work fairly typical of the less classical
side of classicism—the description of nature is of a
thoroughly fantastic kind.   Not merely that it is
informed with human features: but that they are the
features of an artificial type of humanity.   This is
the distinction between what may be called imaginative and fanciful mythology.   The former is the
genuine mythology of a people still in the naïve

stage of growth: and the forms with which it peoples mountain and wood are, like itself, not far removed from the spontaneous and unreflective life of nature which suggested them at first, and which remains when they vanish. The forms of an artificial age, on the contrary, are really more remote from those of naïve humanity than these from the life of flowers and trees. The favourite metaphor for colour—*e.g.* 'blushing'—suggests forcibly the atmosphere of civilised society. We meet with 'blushing flowers,' and 'blushing berries';' and 'blushing Flora paints the enamel'd ground².' The last line suggests the equally characteristic use of processes of art. The reflected woods 'paint the waves' with green: when Alexis 'views his face' in the spring the rising blushes 'paint the wat'ry glass:' and bright flowers and buds when they do not 'blush' rarely fail to wear 'dyes.' So again the larks when they 'leave their little lives in air' are busy 'preparing their notes.' Theirs is not the 'unpremeditated art' of Shelley's *Skylark*, a poem in which what I have called the mythology, though abundant, is of the imaginative not the fantastic kind: the human qualities with which it glorifies the small brown creature carry no discordant suggestions of civilisation.

¹ *Windsor Forest*, 38.

² It is interesting to observe that music has associations distinctly more in accord with nature than those of painting. This seems to be partly because as a matter of history its invention belongs to a more primitive epoch: partly because painting, being primarily imitative, is more decidedly artificial than music, which originated in the spontaneous utterances of feeling.

What is the explanation of this feature of Augustan classicism? For it must be admitted that the arbitrary as such is no part of serious classic art, violating as it does the continuity and order which are of its essence. But it is rare for any actual movement to exhibit in their purity the principles which the historian perceives on the whole to dominate it. The complexity of human nature confounds our hard lines of division: and various conditions of the Augustan age caused it to pursue in one region the same qualities which it rejected with scorn in another. And as this fact is of high importance for clearness, I shall here devote a paragraph to it.

I conceive these conditions to fall under two heads: first. the vigour of a certain form of passion, —hatred,—secondly, the literal imitation of certain foreign models. The latter seriously influenced their conception of the theoretical requirements of classical art: the former often caused them to be violated in practice. Let an Augustan describe men—men as he knows them, moving in the artificial society in which he sees them move, hating one another with the hate of jealous authors, of rival place hunters, of Whig and Tory: men capable of the bitterness of Pope towards Addison or of Lady Mary Wortley Montagu towards Pope :—men, in a word, of the age of the *Dunciad* and of *Gulliver's Travels:* he will display a descriptive boldness not less than that with

which the Romantic poet threads the subtlest laby-
rinths of his imagination. It is needless to illustrate
in detail; a few of Pope's portraits from the *Dunciad*,
Epistle to Arbuthnot and *Satires* would suffice.   On
the other hand, the purity of Augustan classicism
was impaired by a blind imitation which, instead of
translating Greek modes of thought into modern,
inlaid them as it were unaltered in the alien mass.
And so their style receded from Hellenism in proportion as their language·approached it. It was a
habit borrowed from the similar pseudo-classicism of
France.   Nature, which to the Teutonic peoples—at
least to the literary portions of them—had long cast
off the rude and mysterious robe which Teutonic
imagination had cast about her, could not now
assume the alien radiance with which she had appeared in Greece; and to import these Dianas and
Floras and river-gods and wood-nymphs into the
sober landscape of England was as unclassical in
spirit as it was Greek in form.   And then these men
had no more sympathy with the forms which they so
continually used than for the simplicity of nature
which they used them to replace.   Unclassical however as this practice was, it became habitual, until
the movement towards nature, of which Thomson
and Goldsmith and Cowper caught in some degree
the coming dawn, bringing, as we have seen, both
Romantic and classical influences in its train, swept
away with one hand this pseudo-Hellenism, while

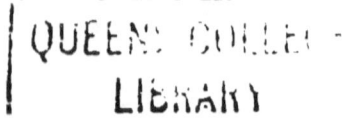

with the other it indirectly fostered that eager adoption in art of all the various material of nature, which was a prime canon of Romantic doctrine and practice. Pseudo-Hellenism was conventional, it was fashionable; but though classic expression is always conventional, it is the permanent, not the transient, element of custom to which it must conform.

§ 20. Finally, to illustrate the action of this principle in that higher region of style,—general construction,—as it affects the proportion and the continuity of the parts. We shall find that it is here the continuity which is chiefly affected. I will select three characteristics.

First, the association of grave and gay. This fantastic combination of the serious and comic must be distinguished from that Shaksperean quality which Schiller described as "the coldness that permits him to joke in the midst of the deepest tragedy." Both are Romantic, inasmuch as the effect of both depends chiefly on contrast: but in the former the end is merely the surprise, in the latter, Schiller notwithstanding, the tragic element derives an enhanced and unique intensity from the transient intervention of the comic. The one might be compared to the alternate shower and sunshine of an April day; the other to the effect sometimes witnessed when in twilight a brief ray of moonlight makes more ghastly the gloom of a thunderstorm. Such is the difference between the easy mingling of these elements in *Henry IV*, *Comedy of Errors*, the *Tempest*, *As you Like it*, or the *Winter's Tale*, and that sterner and subtler genius which sets off with clownish jests the real pathos, touched with art, of Cleopatra's end, or relieves the madness of Lear with the more refined and exquisite jesting of his Fool.   A second characteristic is that air of unreality in the whole circumstances, which is given by the association of different times and countries: as when the bold weavers of Elizabethan England are tormented by mediaeval fairies and make amusement for a king of mythic Athens, or when English squires and knights royster in the country-houses of Illyria; or again where not merely history or geography but general probability suffers playful violence, the whole conception being pointedly fantastic and unreal, as in the forest encounters of the lords of Navarre and the ladies of France, or of the shepherd and courtier lovers among the tongued trees of the Ardennes.   Thirdly, the same arbitrariness appears in particular incidents; *e.g.* the frequency of disguised figures such as the Bellanio of Beaumont and Fletcher, or the Violas, Rosalinds, Celias, Imogens, Portias, the Dromios and Antipholus[1], who figure in the (for the most part earlier[2]) dramas of Shakspere;

---

[1] Of course not forgetting that the peculiar plot of this play has the authority of Plautus and of Menander: we are however too familiar by this time with the paradoxes of the subject to suppose that Greek and Classic are equivalent terms.

[2] *Cymbeline* is probably among the later: it is placed by Prof. Ward 34th in the list (*Hist. of Eng. Drama*, I. 435).

instruments whence the poet blows as it were a
brilliant bubble of illusion which at the climax bursts
and disappears.   Or again, though involving no
mistaken identity the incident itself may have a
fantastic air: the story of the caskets of 'Portia for
example breaks like a breath from the Arabian
Nights upon the more sober atmosphere of com-
mercial Venice[1].   To a yet airier region belong the
hallucinations due to supernatural influence, of which
the typical and immortal instrument is Puck, the
Ate of Romantic comedy as the witches in *Macbeth*
are the *Ate* of Romantic Tragedy.   This touches one
of the points in which the classic and the Romantic
drama are brought very close.   Without refining too
far, or denying that the conception of aberration
from and that of reconciliation with law are proper
to all tragedy whatever, we may assert that the
former is the more characteristic of Romantic, the
latter of classical feeling.   The property of making
men err by distorting their vision, common to so
many mythical figures, to the Greek Ate, to the
Teutonic Puck, and to the Jewish and Christian
Satan,—was most conformable to the genius of Romantic art, though easily absorbed by classicism.
That reconciliation to law on the other hand, that
retracing of the devious path, which is most characteristic of classicism, also intervenes to terminate the

---

[1] As a matter of fact both the minor and the major argument
of this play, as of many others, appear to have an Eastern origin.

H.   5

most daring vagaries of Romantic incident, whether
it appear in the reassertion of the moral law against
Macbeth, or in the return to their right minds which
the 'naughty spirit,' chided, finally accomplishes in
his deluded lovers.

CHAPTER VI.

CONCLUSION.

§ 21. "I do not compare myself in point of imagination with Wordsworth, said Walter Scott, far from it.......But I can see as many castles in the clouds as any man, as many genii in the curling smoke of a steam engine, as perfect a Persepolis in the embers of a sea-coal fire." These phrases,—hardly just perhaps to the realistic side of Scott's imagination,—suggest an approach of the fantastic to the mysterious, which may help us in making the same transition. In both, the immediate sensuous appearance is transcended: but the fantastic is opposed to it as an arbitrary aberration to a primary reality: while mystery implies that that which immediately appears is felt to be in some sort less real than what is dimly imagined. The one is a conscious creation and evokes a poetic delight: the other is believed to be an intuition, and arouses a religious awe. Hence a difference in treatment. The poet

freely represents the objects of his fancy, sparing no
wealth of colour, no industry of pencil: but where
the imagined object is felt to be mysterious, he
shrinks from graphic portraiture and substitutes
obscure hints. He confines himself more to the
immediate presentation, dwells upon the more significant parts of it, repeats them with emphasis or
points to them as it were silently and leaves them.
Hence a profound and dominating sense of mystery
gives a new importance to parts otherwise wholly
subordinate.   It is obvious that we have here under
a new form and arising from a quite different source,
that peculiarly Romantic tendency to exaggeration
of the part which we have already twice encountered.
As before an artistic love of contrast, or a devotion to the variety of nature, drew the part out of
subordination to the whole, so here the sense that
each is implicated in something not itself, gives it a
like undue predominance.

A brief illustration of one phase of this effect
may suffice.   Take these lines of *Christabel.*

> "Is the night chilly and dark?
> The night is chilly, but not dark.
> The thin grey cloud is spread on high,
> It covers but not hides the sky:
> The moon is behind, and at the full:
> And yet she looks both small and dull.
> The night is chill, the cloud is grey."

The very iteration of these simple phrases about
the dull night and the grey cloud has the mysterious

effect which in music is sometimes obtained by the slow repetition of a single note. Merely to dwell upon what seems simple forces the doubt that all is not so simple as it seems: and with this doubt comes conjecture, and with unsatisfied conjecture, wonder and awe.

§ 22. We have now traced through the proposed range the main characteristics of Romantic and Classical style. It has been for the most part a record of deviations from a type of expression which is formally adequate without being redundant, and, in the larger sense of style, from a type of construction in which there is at once *proportion* and *continuity*. On the other hand, in respect to the choice of ideas, we had to recognise another side of the contrast, the deviation from the range of conceptions permitted by a narrow aesthetic and a severe intellectual ideal. The two sides of the opposition are, doubtless, as I have indicated in the first chapter, connected by no essential link: perfection of the formal elements of style is quite compatible with the catholicity of taste which proceeds from extended culture. The form which civilisation demands may still be imposed on ideas which are alien to it. A Hellenic art is possible without Hellenic contempt of the βάρβαροι. Both sides of the contrast we have seen influenced by the fundamental tendencies of Romanticism. We have found the idea of nature, whether as a tendency or as a conscious principle, producing a realism offensive to a narrow aesthetic, or intellectual taste; we have found on the other hand imperfection in form arising either from a love of arbitrariness in art, one phase of which is the proneness to excessive contrast,—or from stress of feeling, or from absorption in the mysterious. Sometimes it is the iteration or the incompleteness of lyric expression, which produces disproportion; sometimes the abruptnesses, the surprises, the startling contrasts of fantastic construction which break the continuity. Nature, as an embodiment of endless variety, art, as selecting the most striking instances of it, and exaggerating them, alike contribute to Romantic effect. Romantic poetry, to exert its full influence, must act on minds not yet trained to demand perfect proportion and continuity; it tells by the splendour and impressiveness of its ideas, rather than by their fitness; by the brilliance of single strokes, not by the harmony of their combination. The Romantic has the power which creates, rather than that which restrains. His is not the curbing strength of the charioteer, but the impulsive and capricious energy of the horse. With the rebelliousness, however, of Ἐπιθυμία, he combines the nobility of Θυμός. In the Romantic the lamp of Power burns with a brilliant and eager light: in the Classic its paler beam is mingled with the rays of the lamp of Sacrifice. And this lamp also never goes out in the chamber of the true artist. Not that

in art, any more than in ethics, rightly understood,
an absolute loss, a final surrender of good is asked or
needed: in both only the undue exaltation of the
part, of the individual, is foregone for the sake of the
society, of the whole : what egoism is in ethics, disproportion is in art.   And so from another side we
come round to the conception of that third stage in
art in which the opposites are combined, and the
exuberance of Romanticism is united with the aus-
terity of Classicism.

> "Mid struggling sufferers, hurt to death, she lay!
> Shuddering, they drew her garments off—and found
> A robe of sackcloth next the smooth white skin.
>
> Such, poets, is your bride, the muse! young, gay,
> Radiant, adorn'd outside; a hidden ground
> Of thought and of Austerity within."

NOTE TO CHAPTER I.

An exhaustive treatment of the subject of Romanticism would require an account of various developments
of it which hardly fell within the scope of an essay
professedly confined, like the present, to the sphere of
literature, and English literature.   It would be necessary,
for example, to describe with what an uproar the wave

which had proceeded from Germany to invade England
and France, broke also upon Italy. It would be necessary
to trace the reflexion of the literary movement in the
music of Schubert and Schumann, and in the painting of
Overbeck and Schadow. It would be necessary to explain the intimate relation in which this aesthetic movement stood with Schelling's philosophy of Nature,—a
relation which resulted from the parallel advance of a
one-sided philosophical development of Kant and a one-
sided literary development of Schiller, who was at the
same time Kant's most eloquent exponent. But the
romantic influence on art and on philosophy was transient;
and it would be necessary, finally, to show how the
movement did in one sphere obtain an abiding though
little recognised influence, by immensely furthering the
adoption of that historical point of view which has led
to so great a revolution in our conception of the past.
But England, never fully mastered by the movements of
the continent,—half convert of the Renascence, imperfect disciple of. the Revolution, absorbing slowly what
attracts its somewhat limited sensibility, and rejecting
rather with the slight impatience of a satisfied curiosity
than with any deep-seated revulsion of passion,—England
felt little these wide-reaching ramifications of Romanticism; or if she felt them, it was as single and separate
movements which scarcely penetrated deep enough to
rouse the consciousness of their common origin.

CAMBRIDGE: PRINTED BY C. J. CLAY, M.A., AT THE UNIVERSITY PRESS.